Extreme

Peculiar Pets

School Specialty
Publishing
Columbus, Ohio

By Teresa Domnauer

Copyright © 2007 School Specialty Publishing, a member
of the School Specialty Family.

Printed in the United States of America. All rights reserved. Except as permitted
under the United States Copyright Act, no part of this publication may be
reproduced or distributed in any form or by any means, or stored in a database or
retrieval system, without prior written permission from the publisher, unless
otherwise indicated.

Library of Congress Cataloging-in-Publication Data is on file with the publisher.

Send all inquiries to:
School Specialty Publishing
8720 Orion Place
Columbus, OH 43240-2111

ISBN 0-7696-4334-5

2 3 4 5 6 7 8 9 10 PHX 10 09 08 07

Many people have pets. Some people have pets that look very different from most!

Afghan Hound

An Afghan hound
is a kind of dog.
It has a long nose
and long, silky hair.

Mini Hedgehog

A mini hedgehog
has pointy quills.
It can roll up
into a ball.

Rat

A rat is a smart
and clean animal.
A pet rat will sit
in its owner's hands.

Chinchilla

A chinchilla is
soft and furry.
It has big round
ears and eyes.

Gray Parrot

A gray parrot is
a large bird.
It can say words
just like a person!

Green Budgie

A green budgie
is a small parrot.
It can learn to sit
on a person's finger.

Potbellied Pig

A potbellied pig has
a big belly and short legs.
It eats a lot.

Chameleon

A chameleon is
a kind of lizard.
Its skin can
change color.

Boa Constrictor

A boa constrictor is
a big snake.
It can weigh up to
50 pounds!

Green Iguana

A green iguana is
a kind of lizard.
It has pointy scales
on its back.

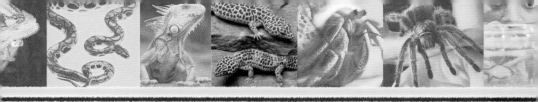

Leopard Gecko

A leopard gecko has
dark spots.
It can live
for 30 years!

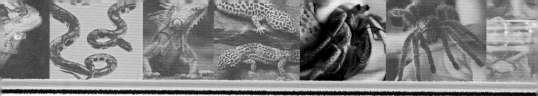

Hermit Crab

A hermit crab has
one big claw.
It finds a shell
and lives inside.

Tarantula

A tarantula is
a hairy spider.
It can be as big
as a hand!

Pet Care

All pets need care.
They need food, water,
and a place to live.
It is good to learn a lot
about a pet before you
bring it home!

EXTREME FACTS ABOUT PECULIAR PETS

- The Afghan hound is known as "the king of dogs" because of its elegant, noble appearance.

- Mini hedgehogs come from Africa.

- Rats can be trained to perform simple tricks, such as running through mazes.

- Chinchillas like to sniff everything around them. They have a very good sense of smell.

- Gray parrots can learn to say hundreds of words.

- Most budgies can learn to talk, similar to parrots.

- The best food for potbellied pigs is pig chow.

- Chameleons' eyes can see forward and backward at the same time.

- A boa constrictor can grow to be 10 feet long, about as long as a car!

- There are over 900 different kinds of iguanas.

- Never hold a gecko by its tail. It will break off!

- Hermit crabs are nocturnal. They sleep during the day and are active at night.

- Fifteen kinds of tarantulas live in the state of Texas.